Break Through to Happiness

your handy little guide to a happier life

Jan Haley Brightwood

Published in 2013 by FeedARead.com Publishing
– Arts Council funded

First Edition January 2013

Second Edition with added content July 2013

A CIP catalogue record for this title is available from the British Library.

That said, Jan Haley Brightwood is happy for passages up to 1000 words to be quoted and credited in any reviews or references to the book or her work. She can be contacted through her website:

breakthroughtohappiness.co.uk

Dedication

This book is dedicated to YOU!

It's *your* book, and it is meant for you to use it. So break free and write in it. To get the most out of it, interact with it. Think of it as a workbook (or better still, a funbook!). Stick yellow (or pink) stickies in it. Fold the corners on pages. Scribble and make notes in the margins, underline and highlight parts that resonate, add your own insights, dreams and intentions.

Happy doodling!

Love Jan x

Happy News!

Great news! The art of happiness can be learned!

So it's open to all of us, no matter what we have believed was possible (or impossible) for us in the past.

Decide, right now, to become a student of Happiness.

What more rewarding subject for study can there be?

Contents

Introduction 7
Snapshot: Chasing My Tail 9
Happy and Healthy 11
Tips for Vitality 13
Snapshot: Fending Off The Inevitable 21
Happy and Wealthy 23
Abundance Tips 25
Snapshot: In Search of Self-Respect 33
Happy in Yourself 35
Tips for Self Love 37
Waking up to the Source of Joy 45
Snapshot: Hanging On to What We'd Got 49
Happy Relationships 51
Tips for Giving Love 53
Snapshot: An End to Rational Tyranny 61
Happy with the Universe 65
Tips for Loving Life 67
A Word About Time 79
Snapshot: From Pushing to Pulling 81
About Jan 83
Further Reading 85

Which Way to Happiness?

"There is no way to
happiness.
Happiness is the way."

in other words:

Happiness is not a destination, it's a way of travelling.

Introduction

That's exactly what this whole little book is - an introduction. It's a quick-to-read, easy to take on, cheery trip through some powerful concepts which transform lives. It's short. It's straightforward. It has suggestions for things you can do immediately.

Would you like to feel a bit happier than you do now? A lot happier? Are you prepared to try out some new ideas to bring more happiness into your life? This is a great place to start. You can read it in a day, or take your time chewing it over in bite-sized chunks. If you're feeling quite happy enough already, thank you very much, then please pass this book on to someone you know who might appreciate a little lift.

As with all books of this nature, it will work best for you if you work with it. Think about how the ideas presented can be applied to your own particular circumstances, and make notes to help you remember. If you keep the book in the loo, keep a pen there too, so you don't miss recording your insights!

I firmly believe that each and every one of us has within us the means to be happy most of the time. *Joy is our natural state.* Here, I'm presenting my personal optimistic and enthusiastic view of the world. I've been on a journey from deep unhappiness to happy every day. I'm delighted to be sharing some of the thoughts and teachings that have helped (and continue to help) me to live a happier life.

When we take control of our own happiness levels, we empower ourselves to move towards the life we want.

What Happiness Means to Me

Snapshot: Chasing My Tail

I was always running, running, running.

Running to the station, anxious about missing the train. Running from the station to catch a bus. Running from the bus to open up our shop in Colchester.

Running upstairs if there was a lucky gap between customers, to fetch stock, to nip to the loo, to grab a bite to eat.

Running from the shop to the station again, not wanting to miss the only connection. Often standing on the hour-long journey back to Norwich.

I was eating the healthiest foods, on a pH-balancing plan, with no caffeine, no sugar, very little meat and no wheat. I was the slimmest I'd ever been, but I wasn't well. I had osteoarthritis in my neck and was frequently felled by migraines.

My intention for the diet was not to lose weight. I was trying to boost my immune system to prepare for having all of my metal fillings removed. I'd read that mercury in the amalgam was linked to headaches, anxiety and depression. Desperate to find a way out of the depression that had gripped me for years, I was willing to put myself through quite an ordeal. Hours in the dentist's chair, with a vitamin C intravenous drip. Everyone working around me wearing protective masks, to filter the toxic heavy metal from the air they were breathing, while they were drilling out my metal fillings. I had a mouth full of them.

In the seventies, there were dentists who came around the schools. I remember the drilling, acutely, but I don't remember having any problem with my teeth before that. Were they perhaps paid by the filling?

My lovely Mam came with me, keeping me company for the four days of treatment. I have nice white porcelain fillings now, cast to fit my teeth. I kept on that healthy food plan for a long time, maybe another year or so, then gradually slid into some bad habits again. But I've maintained many of the good ones.

Did removing my fillings end my depression and get rid of the migraines? There was no immediate discernable effect. But I'm jolly glad not to have that mercury leaking into my system any more. Taking that important step opened the way for me to begin to rise out of my 'victim' mentality and take control of my life, my health and my happiness.

Happy and Healthy

Love it or not, this body of yours is where you happen to be, for this lifetime anyway! It makes no sense at all to abuse it. But how do we get to be happy and healthy?

Happiness 'substitutes' like over-eating, over-drinking or excessive drug use only put us in a bind that ultimately heaps more unhappiness on us and those who love us. Most of us manage to avoid the worst excesses, but give in to a lot of temptations and end up feeling less than satisfied with our body shape and health.

How to maintain a 'healthy-enough' body, and be happy about how we're doing it, is a big question. I hope some of the answers offered here will help you on your way to a happy relationship with your true home: your body!

May your health blossom and bloom.

Happy Thoughts

Tips for Vitality

These are my personal favourite suggestions, collected from a variety of sources and experimentation. I hope you may find them helpful. I'm not a health professional, though. Always do your own research and learn to follow your inner wisdom about what's best for you.

No 1: love and appreciate your body

Chances are there's something you really don't like about your body. It's quite likely there are several areas with which you're less than satisfied. You might even go so far as to admit that you hate certain things about it. It's easy to guess that, because we all have these insecurities to a greater or lesser degree. If you are truly committing yourself to finding happiness, you must leave these negative body views behind.

Try considering this. Whatever you think is 'wrong' with it, without your body you would be - literally - nowhere! You'd be no more than a wisp of joy on the wind. Happy, I'm pretty certain, but not having a Life.

Your body is what is providing you with a Life. There are 30+ trillion tiny cells cooperating to get you about and act out your will. That in itself is astonishing! Your body is a fantastic achievement of evolution. It's your home for this Lifetime and it totally belongs to you! Not only that, but it's totally your responsibility, too. So instead of blaming your body for not being whatever image of perfection you've wished for, it's time to turn things around and celebrate the awesome wonder that it is.

Try starting each day by getting quiet, for a couple of minutes at least, and giving silent thanks for all the things about your body that are working. When you feel ready to, start sending the good feelings you have about the parts that are working, or parts you're proud of, to those parts you're less than happy with. Give thanks for those things too. Keep the good feelings flowing to the parts you've been having issues with.

Do this every day, even if it's just for a couple of minutes.

To embed a new habit, do it for 30 days. Give it 30 days, and see if you start feeling a change. Be aware, the changes may not be what you expected!

No 2: become curious about health

Activate your interest. You want to be happy, right? Isn't that why you're here? And being happy with an unhealthy body is a lot more difficult than being happy with a healthy one.

So, if you don't already explore this area, learn about health. If you have a computer and can go online, it's so easy, just a few clicks away! Otherwise, there are plenty of books, magazines and TV programs all about health. What's a balanced diet? How much exercise do we need? Is coffee really the villain or not? How much alcohol is OK? Are supplements necessary? Are prescription drugs the only way to healing?

You'll find that opinions vary widely. That's OK, that's humanity for you! Always debating. Keep an open mind. Think about who profits from the answers, and whether you trust them. Don't get stressed about the differences of opinion, once you've read more widely you'll begin to get a feeling for which ideas resonate best with you. Follow those and see how it feels. Life is an experiment.

No 3: find the right foods for you

There are certain universal truths. Fresh food is better for you (but not if it's covered with chemicals, always wash fruit and vegetables and choose organic food if possible). Processed food is really only a temporary fix; unfortunately busy people have come to see it as the norm.

No-one is going to thrive on pies and chips and plastic bread. No-one is going to thrive eating mechanically extracted meat from animals which have had terrible, unnatural lives. High sugar and high salt content is going to put enormous strain on all those good chemical factories of ours - our bodies' cells.

Basically, the less tampered with the food is, the better for you it will be.

Having said all that, there is still enormous scope for you to discover and create food that you love, from fresh ingredients that will nourish you and boost your vitality. Don't just dismiss areas you've tried once or never before. Get experimental. Make experimenting with food a fun part of every day - at least until you find enough healthy favourites to keep you and your body happy.

No 4: discover exercise you enjoy

Exercising is important, but if you're going to hate every minute of it, and dread it beforehand, the stress chemicals produced by those negative emotions are going to undo the potential good you're trying to achieve. And anyway, the point is to be happy!

So don't do some sort of "exercise regime" just because you think you "should". Use your imagination to search for, or invent, an activity you will enjoy.

One of my favourites is to turn my music up a little and boogie for a few tracks, as I'm apt to sit at my computer for too long otherwise. Dancing to joyful music is uplifting as well. I'm usually in an even better mood when I get back to work.

Even a brisk walk, every day, is far better than no exercise at all. So make it something you look forward to by finding the most attractive route you can and really noticing beauty around you.

Listening to educational or motivational audios while exercising can be great, as you're getting something else done that you otherwise may not get time for. I used to listen to Tony Robbins while I was on the 'lateral thigh trainer' at home. Boy, was I pumped up mentally and physically at the end of that half hour! Phooh! Watch out world, here I come!

No 5: don't forget to rest

I don't necessarily mean vegging out in front of the box. A lot of TV is just dulling the senses, and a lot more is filling your mind with negativity, especially dramas like soaps. Watch something uplifting, or turn it off. You're in control of what nourishment you're giving to your mind and emotions.

Do you get a good night's sleep? If not, don't put up with it. Depression, anxiety and low motivation get linked into a spiral with lack of sleep. Do some research and explore ways to improve your sleep patterns.

If you're the type of person who carries a lot of tension - let's face it, most of us are these days - explore ways of releasing that. Get a massage. Learn about meditation. Play some soothing music and let yourself float. Free your mind from the daily worries - declare this special half-hour or so your 'worry-free zone' so that your body has a chance to release the tensions.

Take a deep breath, at any time of day, and as you breathe out, relax everything and say, "Aaaaaah!" like a big, happy sigh. I love that one. It's so simple.

No short-cut

There is no short-cut to a healthy body, so you might as well make the effort to ensure that the healthy habits you're beginning to adopt are fun for you. For example, if you hate lettuce, either find a way to make lettuce fun (by snipping it up tiny with the scissors and combining it with grated carrot, grated cheese, balsamic vinegar and olive oil, perhaps) or choose a different green vegetable that you love.

Don't let yourself be defeated, your options are only as limited as your curiosity and imagination. So get creative, because it's out of creativity that the fun in life comes.

I wish you much joy on your route to great health.

What are the benefits that being healthy will bring me?

What values will being healthy satisfy?

My Healthy Intentions

I am finding fun ways to be healthy.

I am enjoying my exercise.

I am loving the healthy food I am eating.

I am filled with vitality and enthusiasm.

Snapshot: Fending Off The Inevitable

It was a phone call I'd made many times before. The claws in my gut were no less tight, for that. Everything depended on a successful outcome. The continuation of our business. Hanging on to our home. And even, in the background, not wanting to acknowledge it, our two-decade relationship. I couldn't imagine it surviving the collapse of everything in our world. I couldn't imagine us getting back into love from being re-housed, humbled, seeing ourselves as failures.

So, once again, I gathered myself to phone a credit card company and arrange a balance transfer. No more than a delaying tactic, always pushing the growing debt ahead of us, in the hope that our business would surge free of its financial difficulties into unbridled success.

Taking on a persona of cheery confidence, I tapped out the number, wading through the 'press one, press two' options, until I had a real person to impress. Not that I needed to impress, it's all done by statistics. And yes, they could offer me a deal, and yes, I took it happily, and yes, another £15 grand rolled over from one card to another.

And, once again, I came off the phone both relieved and sickened. *"When will we ever get out of this bind?"*

Uplifting Ideas

Happy and Wealthy

We've all heard it. "Money can't make you happy, but it helps."

It's my firm belief that the pursuit of money can make you, and others around you, very unhappy indeed. That's not to say money is bad, but it certainly can cloud the issue and there are ways to prioritise what's really of value in life, without money being top of the list.

For example, if the pursuit of money takes so much of your time and energy that you miss your kids growing up, might you not look back after they've left home and wonder if you got the balance right? How about having a family life as well, while you can?

The ideas around making money and how to attract wealth into your life are going through a paradigm shift. While the profit-addicts in control of the corporations are still operating in a system based on scarcity, a new belief system is blossoming, based on abundance, or sufficiency.

Happy hunting and may abundant blessings rain upon you from sunshiny skies!

Joyful Notions

Abundance Tips

I am not a money expert. I know nothing about investment. I am only just learning to have a completely different relationship to wealth myself - and it's blowing my mind! So here, I'm sharing what I'm learning right now. We can experiment together!

No 1: get your priorities right

Of course, there are no "right" or "wrong" answers to this one, there are just choices to be made. Look at your life as a whole. Are you allowing time for the things that really matter to you? If money didn't have to come into the picture at all, ask yourself what are the things you value and in what order? Make a list, play with it. What's missing? What would you like to add? What, when you really think about it, would you drop? Include time with people you love, activities you'd enjoy. What would make you feel fulfilled?

Write a description of a life you would love to be living. What would a day in your ideal life look like in, say, five years time? Write it in the present tense. A great way to do this is to write a letter from your future self, describing all the things you're doing and how you made your new abundant lifestyle come about. This acts like a 'future pull' towards what you really want in life.

Why not aim for that? Why not focus on that, rather than things that you're dissatisfied with?

This is your life - you get to design it. The clearer the picture of what you want, the greater the chances of you getting there (and by the way, your ideal life picture can change - keep playing with it, it's fun to be imagining it, anyway!).

We can't get to where we want to be if we haven't worked out what that is. That's why so many who do earn lots of money are still unhappy. They thought money would make them happy, but money is not the thing. It's what money can enable, that is the thing. We need to have clear pictures of what that is, for each of us, personally, and sail our ships in that direction.

If you're in a partnership or marriage, you both need to do this. If your pictures are wildly different you need to work out a way of bringing them together so that you both feel happy and fulfilled, or you may find your relationship torn apart further down the line. Or you may both be just a bit unhappy all the time.

No 2: see money differently

Money has no worth in and of itself. It is a promissory note - a promise. It works because when we receive money in exchange for something of real value that we've given - like our time or a useful object - we trust that someone else will be prepared to receive that money from us for something we want.

Money is a facilitator. Having money will only add to your happiness if you use it to do the things that you enjoy! So don't allow yourself to be side-tracked into seeing earning money as the big goal, and spending it as compensation for all the time and effort you put in to earn it. That's a treadmill - you will not get any closer to happiness that way.

Money is a tool, a technology, and like a hammer or a bulldozer it is neither good nor evil, but may be put to good or evil use. You are responsible for how the money in your life is used. Use it well. Feel good about how you're using it. Circulate it in a way that fits with how you want the world to be.

No 3: abundance, not scarcity

Our society teaches us that we live in a world where there is not enough to go around, where you have to struggle to stay ahead of the rest, that if I have a lot someone else will have less.

These are beliefs reinforced by the vested interests that wish to keep the population as wage-slaves, "consuming" products and paying taxes to pay interest on money that was conjured out of thin air as debt.

Great news! These beliefs are simply not true! Look around. Wherever nature has the slightest chance to show her colours, there is abundance. Count the berries in the hedgerow. Count the sardines in one shoal! Leaves on a tree .... grains of sand on the beach ...

Abundance is the natural order. We warp the natural order by insisting everything has to be measured by its "monetary value" (remember, money has no value in and of itself). The system tells us that if there is no profit in it, a thing is worthless. This devalues the natural abundance of our beautiful Earth and it devalues and marginalises people who stand in the way of profit.

There is plenty for all. We can feed everyone. We need not strip the rainforests. We simply need to reorganise. Thankfully, there are now brave souls everywhere standing up to change the way we do things.

See the abundance around you and realise: you are a child of Earth and it is your right to use the abundance provided by Earth in the course of living your life. What else could you do? It is every other human being's right too, in equal measure.

Stop thinking there's not enough. We live in abundance, and it's astonishingly beautiful.

No 4: tithe

Tithing is an ancient idea which has been abused in the past, because it became a kind of tax. In essence it is that you freely and with a generous heart give one tenth of your income to worthy causes.

The act of giving to a higher purpose, other than the satisfaction of your own needs, not only makes you feel good, because it's a contribution to wider society, it also stimulates the law of attraction. But it needs to be done with your full blessing, not reluctantly, and not purely with what you will get back in mind! Most people are giving something regularly to various charities - check in with yourself. Are you giving joyously or from guilt? Are you feeling that you can't really afford what you're giving, so there's a little bit of discomfort associated? That's acting out of a belief of scarcity. Are you giving in the spirit of wishing the world a better place? Send good wishes with your gifts.

Remember we live in a world of abundance. Give freely, give generously, and the universe will provide generously for you. If you're starting out with no money, give things. Most of us have heaps of stuff hoarded because we 'might find it useful' one day. Move it on to where it could be useful now, and have faith that what you need will come to you as you need it.

No 5: save a little

In these times of currency uncertainties, I'm not sure of the value of having savings in currency. But as I said, I am definitely not an expert! If you have large savings and investments, my suggestion is to dig deep into the advice available (and not necessarily the establishment advice!) because it would be a tragedy if you woke up one morning to find your hard-earned savings worth a fraction of what they were yesterday, should your currency suddenly lose its value.

Having never had savings myself, I can't say if this works. But the suggestion is that if you have money, you get more. What I'm hearing is keep a little, so that it mounts up a little, but keep circulating the rest. Because it is the flow of money that facilitates what you want to do and be in life, not the hoarding of it.

New paradigm

These ideas may seem controversial; they may even cause emotional responses, because they are challenging the entrenched beliefs of our age.

Allow yourself to feel angry or afraid, if that's your first response. But try to examine where that emotion may be coming from. The call to change is challenging, especially the call to change the filters through which we see the world.

The way to a happier life is to change how we see things.

I wish you all that you could wish for yourself in this wonderful experiment called Life.

What are the benefits that being wealthy will bring me?

What values will being wealthy satisfy?

My Abundance Intentions

I am attracting to me all the resources I need.

I am able to do, what I need to do, when I need to do it.

I am able to share because I have more than enough.

I am feeling money as a flow through my life and directing that flow to good use.

Snapshot: In Search of Self-Respect

Counselling took an awful lot out of me. Not giving it, but getting it.

My counsellor was really great. I think, in other circumstances, we'd have got on well, but *boy* did she make me *work*. I mean, I had to do *all* the talking. She hardly added a thing!

I used to come away trembling, having dug deep. Was it too deep? Who knows? It was part of the process. At times it seemed very self-indulgent. I hoped it was going to help.

One of my main realisations was how dependent I was on approval from others. And I'd take it however it came. If only shallow reasons were available, well, then, shallow reasons would do.

So I resolved to put something else in place. I would create reasons for me to respect myself.

It took a while. Things happen slowly when you're depressed, if they happen at all.

Eventually I started doing some little 'taster' courses with the Open University. I had done pretty well at school, and I liked that about myself. I valued it. So I reasoned, if I did well at some academic stuff again, I'd feel better about myself.

Peering at my fat textbook on the crowded train home, from Colchester to Norwich, a man next to me asked what I was studying. As I began to tell him about the course, 'Fossils and the History of Life', my whole being lit up. I could see the light reflected in his face, in his engaged smile. He commented on my enthusiasm, was inspired by it.

I heard myself telling him, "It's as if half of me has been asleep for twenty years and I didn't even realise it."

I'd rediscovered my passion for learning, and specifically my passion for biology. The study of *life*. I *loved* it.

You might say, my lights were back on.

Happy in Yourself

I believe this is the key. You have the ability to be happy, to generate joy, inside you, right now. You can learn to turn it on like a fountain which will change your life and brighten the day of those you come into contact with.

What makes this difficult is the great crowd of limiting beliefs ingrained in us since childhood. We need to shed the beliefs that hold us back and there are many ways to approach this.

Start with an area that seems appropriate to you. Be patient. Don't be hard on yourself if the first few attempts don't work as well as you hoped. Keep going, because the rewards are immense when you get to your breakthrough moments.

I wish you many joyful twists and turns on your journey of self-discovery.

Happy travelling.

Fun Dreams

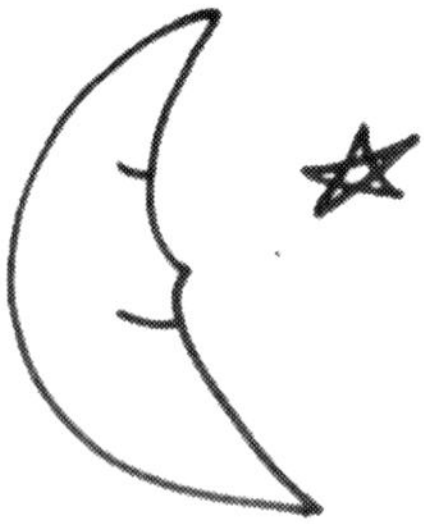

Tips for Self Love

I believe this is the starting point for all happiness. You must start with yourself. When you learn to love yourself, everything else in life is easier, brighter, more harmonious. It is often said we cannot give what we do not have. Find that inner source of joy, and you will be so much more able to bring joy to others.

No 1: self-nurturing is not selfish

Are you kind or cruel to yourself?

If you insist that work is more important than play, that stuff must get done rather than that life is to be lived, or that everyone else comes first, my suggestion is to really question whether this form of prioritising is actually giving you the sort of life you want. Is it making you happy? You set your life's priorities. You can change them.

Take some time to nurture yourself. Many of us are so concerned with what needs to be done, we don't really learn how to find out what we really want in life. What are the important things to you? Is it work? Or is it connection? Are you harsh with your body, expecting more than it can healthily give? Are you harsh with your heart, believing that kindness to yourself is just being soft? Do you believe that discipline is the way to move things forward, rather than encouragement?

A happy person is a self-motivated person. There's no need to be cruel or harsh with yourself. If you've been that way in the past, try a new way now. There certainly can't be any harm in seeing how it goes!

No 2: boost your self-image

What is your inner voice telling you about yourself?

If you give yourself a hard time about every little shortcoming or tell yourself that you're useless or bad or don't deserve happiness, then it's going to be very difficult indeed to create happiness in your life. If this sounds like you, even if it's just for some of the time, then perhaps it would be worth examining where those ideas have come from. Are they true? Of course they're not true! You are an amazing, unique expression of the universe. You have everything inside you to generate beauty and light in your own unique way. That's why you're here. So it's time to change the way you talk to yourself. Make it positive and encouraging instead of beating yourself up or putting yourself down.

Dare to imagine yourself free of fear, free of the restriction of what others expect or demand of you. Picture yourself the way you'd like to be. Play with the notion, imagine yourself in different ways, different roles, different situations. What feels good? Follow that notion. Take little steps in the direction of this new you. If it feels good, do more of that!

No 3: drop the blame-game

We've all been conditioned to look at the other person and decide it's their fault. "My father never encouraged me", "my mother makes me feel guilty", "my sisters are so bitchy". This is playing the victim role. If you really want to be happy, drop the blame-game altogether. Your family, friends and colleagues are all dealing with their stuff. Time for you to let them get on with it and face your own.

Take responsibility for your moods. The emotions

you feel in interactions with others are your emotions; other people don't give them to you, you generate them yourself. You can learn to detach from the emotions that wash through you automatically when others 'press your buttons', you can treat them as information instead. Eventually you can learn to generate different, beneficial emotions, even when people are doing things that used to annoy you or knock you off balance before. This is how you get into the driving seat for your own beautiful life's journey.

No 4: drop the drama

Stop creating drama around the circumstances of your life. You're not acting in a soap. Take time to think about whether this 'huge' thing you're getting so upset about really is all that important after all. If you sit quietly for a while and reflect on what's truly important to you (especially if you're working on dropping the blame-game!) you may well decide that the relationship is more important than the fuss you wanted to create. Having said that, if, on deep reflection, you believe you are being badly used, consider either stating your case in a calm, adult way or moving on to more beneficial relationships.

Listen to the stories you tell yourself about what happens in your life. Is it really all as bad as you make out? If you decide not to get upset about them, do the issues just fade away?

No 5: balance

We all want to love and be loved. We want to be useful and appreciated, we want to feel important to someone else. It's important to strike a balance between how much we do for others, and how much we do for ourselves.

Giving - whether it is time, affection, thoughtful gifts or physical help - is a wonderful thing and should never be undervalued. But if we're only giving to others and never to ourselves, pretty soon we're running on empty. That's when we can begin to feel martyr-ish, so resentments build, tempers flare. Or, if those emotions remain unexpressed, illness eventually expresses them for us.

Never thinking about others, living in our own little bubble, cannot lead to happiness either. We are social creatures, it's how we've evolved. If we cut ourselves off from others, especially those close to us, we're missing the loving connections that make life so sweet. The pleasure to be gained from a simple act of kindness is immense, and it's been scientifically proven that the giver, the receiver and any witnesses to an act of kindness all benefit emotionally and physically too!

No 6: do a little of what you love

Take time every day to do a little of what you love. It doesn't need to have any other purpose than that you enjoy it. Bake, paint, garden, play music, dance, knit, make a mosaic, take photographs, make something from wood, go birdwatching, run, skip, read - whatever it is that YOU love to do. If you didn't have time yesterday - make time today!

Giving ourselves permission to do something - regularly - simply for the joy of doing it, is a simple and instant way to bring happiness into our lives. This is how we re-energise and feed our souls.

And the knock on effect will be a smiling you, bringing happiness into your loved ones' lives too.

No 7: quiet time

Make space in your life for quiet time. A space where you can be calm and at peace, where you can drop all the stories, cease all your struggles and just suspend yourself from the worries of life. One of the simplest ways to do this is to go for a walk (without your phone!). Find the most natural surroundings. If you're in a city, go to a park, or choose avenues where there are trees. Notice colours, textures, smells, sounds. Listen to birdsong. For me, birdsong is one of the most divine gifts on Earth, an instant reminder of the natural beauty available to us if we just focus on it.

Learning meditation is immensely beneficial. Meditation has been shown to give amazing physical, mental and emotional benefits to those who practice regularly.

It's my direct experience that we have inside us a joy generator. We can learn to release this endless source of joy and love from within, without depending on anyone else to give us anything. It's the most beautiful gift to humanity and every single person on the planet has it available to them. It's like we've been feeling impoverished while we sat on a box full of treasures. If you have no hint of this yet, don't despair. Just take little steps, take action to brighten your way of looking at life and your way of relating to others. You have it, it's there, one day it will burst through like the sun coming out from behind a cloud.

Connecting to this inner resource on a regular basis improves all aspects of life - relationships, health, emotional balance, intellectual and problem solving capabilities, the ability to create abundance - everything!

What are the benefits that being happy to be me will bring?

What values will being happy to be me satisfy?

My Self-Love Intentions

I am giving myself space to be who I really am.

I am doing what I love.

I am here to be joyful and to bring joy to others.

Waking up to the Source of Joy

It can be difficult to 'feel the joy' through the fuzzy head and stiff body that I have shortly after waking up.

A deep breath and "Aaaaaah" immediately helps - allowing the joy rather than summoning it. Surrender rather than struggle. And here it comes .... so beautiful.

**I am, in this moment, enough.
I have enough. There is enough.
We are, all, enough. Earth
provides enough. It is all here,
now. Here it is.
Here I am.**

"Aaaaaah!"

Joy, emanating from the area of the heart, spilling out through the body, so all parts feel the joy. Even my hands and feet feel the deep peace and pleasure of this joy.

Emanating from the area of the heart, yet also from somewhere so deep within my being, it has nothing to do with my physical body. It is deeper in than the physical body. It appears from 'no place', from a reality so much more profound, and then it affects my body.

This joy, this love, available on tap to everyone at any time, emanates from 'no-where' then triggers the physical sensations in the body. Those are the mechanisms that evolution has given us so that we can experience this joy in the physical plane. These sensations are not the joy any more than my body is me. They are not the joy any more than the fuel is the motion, or the vehicle is the driver.

I am not my body - I have a body.
I am not my mind - I have a mind.
I am not my emotions - I have emotions.
I am not my personality -
I have a personality.

We "drive around" in our bodies and, if we care to access it, we have an unlimited supply of high energy joy-fuel available to us, in our connection to the divine Source of all things.

The body needs food and water to keep functioning. The soul needs a regular connection to Spirit, which connects us to everything and everyone. The soul needs this connection to thrive and grow and to motivate the human personality in the course of a lifetime.

And it's wonderfully simple and beautiful to access this astounding, endless supply of Life Juice! I am so thankful to have been shown this.

A simple way to stimulate your joy generator

Quiet your mind. Don't struggle with it. Breathe deeply. Imagine breathing into your heart. Release all those niggling thoughts in your head. They're not important. Life is an experiment. What is, is.

After each deep breath, as you exhale, say, "Aaaaaah" like a big fat happy sigh. After three deep breaths, take a few smaller breaths until your breathing is calm and back to normal. Then do three deep breaths again.

Breath into your heart. Feel your heart expand. Drop your attention from your mind, your tangle of thoughts, to your heart. Here, there are no thoughts with words, only a profound knowing. Heart-knowing.

Allow the skin of the skull to relax. Give the mind five minutes 'off'. Place yourself in the care of your heart, your centre of love and joy. Imagine your 'you-ness' dropping from your head into your heart. Put all your attention on your breathing, on your heart expanding. Imagine housing yourself there, in your great big beautiful heart.

"Aaaaaah." Give thanks to your amazing heart, which beats the pulse of Life through you, unceasingly.

If you're not yet feeling the joy, put one hand over your heart area, smile, and say, gently, "Allow." Keep smiling. Keep saying "Allow" and relaxing more with each out-breath, "Aaaaaah".

This is all about 'taking yourself off the hook' for a few moments, taking attention away from all the clamouring thoughts, from the 'stuff, stuff, stuff to sort'. It's about allowing the joy some space to come through.

It's yours. It's there. Right now. Available, right now. Do this every day. Do it any time of day! You will begin to notice some differences.

Once you're happy with doing this regularly, there are many kinds of meditations you can try.

I wish you the deep joy of connection.

More Happy Thoughts

Snapshot: Hanging On to What We'd Got

"We don't bring each other joy any more."

Who wants to hear those words from their lifetime partner? But, in part at least, the words rang painfully true.

We worked six days a week and on the seventh day we'd not the energy to go out and do something joyful together. Anyway, there was the washing and shopping and cleaning and domestic this and that to get done. And through it all, the constant worry.

Running a business together is tough on couples. You're never off-duty, any time can become a work meeting about logistics, issues that need discussing or just information that needs to be passed on. After a few years we tried to have a rule – *not after nine at night*. That still left precious little time free of business pressures.

The truth is, in the desperate measures we were taking to try to make our business a success, we lost sight of what was important in our relationship. You can't do that and keep the love alive. You can't shelve the joy, postpone the fun, to come back to when you're less stressed, when you have more time.

Still, we'd been best friends, close confidantes, partners in everything, for a very long time. We hung on, believing it would all right itself once the business became a success. Or hoping so.

Eventually, it was clear that wasn't going to work. So, heartbroken, after 23 years, we made the break.

We didn't desert each other though. We helped each other while our business went down the pan. We supported each other through the bankruptcy. And from the moment we'd decided to part, there were no recriminations. No analysis. No blame. My partner led the way in that and I'll always be grateful that he set such a powerful standard straight away.

I'm so thankful and proud that we managed it like that. And that's why we're still such good friends now.

Happy Relationships

We're all aware of how important relationships are to our happiness. Humans are social animals, we need to love and be loved, we need to contribute and to feel appreciated.

All too often, though, we trip ourselves up by failing to understand the other person or just becoming complacent. Or we give too much and end up feeling used.

Some people are seriously lacking in self-love and this makes it very difficult for them to find a loving partner, or to receive love when it's offered. For those, perhaps the section on how to be happy in yourself would be the best place to focus for a while.

Some people are so selfish that their partners often feel invisible. It should be fairly clear that if you don't give any thought to what the other people in your life need or want, your relationship with them will suffer. But sometimes it's just a lack of awareness rather than a wish to be unkind.

It's all a question of balance. My own experience is that relationships work best if you come together as people who are already happy, and then you share that happiness with each other in a loving and caring way. If you are unhappy and looking to another to fill the void for you, you're very likely to be disappointed.

You may be in a floundering relationship that you want to save, or a fairly contented partnership that you want to juice up.

It is my hope that these pages offer plenty of scope to help you improve the way you relate to others, so that everyone is happier.

Wishing you much love.

Tips for Giving Love

I'm not a relationship expert, but I've been in a few. In my younger days, I was all over the place, on every corner of the triangle. Happily I've been lucky enough to remain great friends with my ex-partner who I've never stopped loving and I'm enjoying a new rich, joyful, perfectly matched relationship now too.

I certainly don't always get it 'right', but I'm genuinely trying to do better and to learn from my mistakes. I think that's probably what we really want from each other, that we're trying and learning, while we're supporting and loving.

Here are some suggestions and observations which have helped me so far.

No 1: first, love yourself

This can be so difficult to grasp, because in our culture someone who acts superior or smug or vain is disliked and labelled: "he really *loves himself*, doesn't he?" We're taught that having a high opinion of ourselves (and a low opinion of others) is bad and that this is the same as loving yourself.

This is simply not true. It is not the same at all. Self-love and self-nurture are not like selfishness or arrogance. It's enough to say here that without loving yourself, whether consciously or subconsciously, you feel undeserving of love from others, and this will colour all your relationships.

If you're happy in yourself, happy with who you are, then you will bring happiness to others and they will love you for it!

No 2: come together as happy people

Have fun together. Make fun a real priority. Make the ordinary things fun to do, together.

It's a simple concept, although it's not always easy to 'do'. If you want to be happy in your relationships, be happy when you're with people.

Take responsibility for the mood you're in. No-one "puts" you in a mood, you put yourself there with the responses that you choose and the thoughts you have about stuff. Step out of the victim mode - believing that life happens to you and blaming others for your circumstances - and make the decision that you're going to take control of yourself and this life of yours. Learn about emotions, where they come from, and how you can master them. You will then become the driver of your own life, instead of just the passenger with your Life-Car on some sort of emotion-driven auto-pilot.

Tell your partner and other significant people in your life that you are making the effort to change, to become a happier person and you're hoping for their support. Don't be discouraged if they don't believe you - if you've been a grumpy person they'll probably need to see some real results before they cheer!

If you make a consistent effort and over time it feels totally one-sided, you might want to consider finding happier people to be happy with.

No 3: check your expectations

Oh, how disappointment hurts! How it burns! Disappointment arises from thwarted expectations, but are our expectations always fair?

If you often feel disappointed, try really examining whether your expectations of others - and of yourself - are reasonable. If you adjusted them, might you and your loved ones be able to enjoy life, and each other, a bit more, with less pressure? Are your 'rules for life' really about the important things, or could you let a few of them go?

If you feel your partner (or child, parent, sibling, flatmate ... you get the idea!) falls short most of the time, try a week where you make no demands on them. Try just giving love and encouragement all week. Don't judge their behaviour, don't put them down. How does it feel to give, unconditionally?

Isn't that the kind of support we'd all love to have from each other? We can only get it by giving it.

No 4: keep communications flowing

Nagging and sniping, sulking and flaring are all counter-productive and immature forms of communication.

Form an agreement with your loved ones that you want to be able to let each other know about feelings and events in a level, adult way without Mount Vesuvius erupting or another Ice Age gripping the household. We each need to take responsibility for our own reactions and calm them down.

Communication means listening, too! Learn about active listening. Often we think we're listening, but what we're actually doing is rehearsing in our minds what we're about to say ourselves, or we're paying more attention to our own thoughts about what's being said, which can drown out the speaker's actual meaning.

Blessed are the flexible, for they shall not be bent out of shape. Remember this, you're not always right. And you're not always wrong. Be prepared to change your mind or compromise (but not all the time!). Right or wrong, both parties in a relationship need to be heard and understood, otherwise it's more of a dictatorship! Being kind may get happier results than being right.

No 5: be a safe haven

Be a safe place for your loved one to be him or her Self. Don't mock or judge, especially when they are opening up to you. If you want honesty from your partner, you must make it safe for them to be honest. You must be ready and willing to forgive if they've slipped up.

This doesn't mean allowing yourself to become subservient to the other, to be abused or bullied, to be repeatedly overlooked in the relationship. In those circumstances, by all means forgive if you can, it will be better for you, but get yourself safely out of there (get a friend to be with you). You are a shining light and you deserve the joy of love in equal partnership. Believe that, and seek it.

Let your loved one know you intend to be a safe haven for them, and that you expect the same from them. Forgive yourself if you slip up occasionally. It's all about trying to do it better, and loving each other in the trying.

No 6: we are divine

Look into the eyes of your loved one, especially when you're both laughing. What do you see? What an amazing light there is there. What an awesome spark of Life.

When I see that in the eyes of my beloved, I see the beautiful light within him, his beautiful soul-light. I see divinity. I am loving his unique, quirky, human personality and I am loving that which is eternal in him. Seeing the evolutionary impulse lighting up his being, seeing that he is so much more than the body and the personality of this particular lifetime, my love and reverence for him deepens even more.

You can feel it, too. Doesn't the room feel different when your loved one is there? Totally different to when it's just you? You feel the presence of another divine being, another Life. You feel a connection with them. And often, you can feel that connection when they're somewhere else entirely. It's not just the body that you connect with.

I know that my love has all the resources he needs within him, he needs nothing from me, and I need nothing from him. I meet him knowing that I am also energy and light, a drop in the ocean of all that is. We love to come together in joy and celebrate the joy we bring.

Knowing that a part of us is eternal and that we are joined there, inseparable there, helps us to detach from the often petty concerns of daily life and get a perspective on what is really important.

I wish you joyous and sparkling relationships.

What are the benefits that having happy relationships will bring me?

What values will having happy relationships satisfy?

My Loving Intentions

I am feeling compassion for others.

I see the divine in my loved ones.

I am bringing joy to my relationships.

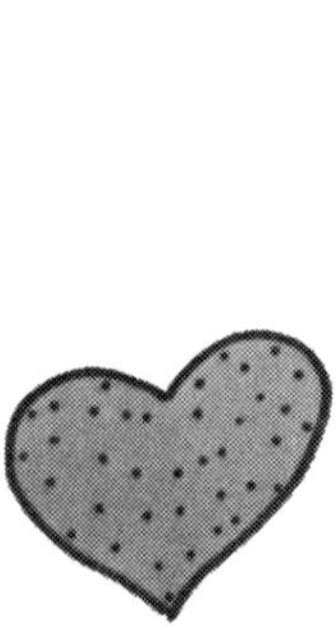

Snapshot: An End to Rational Tyranny

I heard someone say they'd read enough self-help books to stack up and jump off.

I could relate to that. Right through my depression, I'd had phases like that. In fact, I was always interested in what made people behave or feel the way they did. I learned a lot about what causes what, what experiences set up what hang-ups, what vicious circles maintain unhelpful behaviours … knowing that stuff doesn't help you shake it off, though. Thinking you *should* be able to act differently, now that you understand, can actually just lead to increased self-criticism, increased anxiety, even deeper depression.

"Why can't I get out of this?"

So what did it take to get me out of it? Anthony Robbins' audio course, 'Lessons in Mastery' was helping, but it took something outside of the rational framework I was stuck in, to finally set me free. I was lucky enough to be dating a hypnotherapist. Not just any hypnotherapist – one of the best.

What it took was some direct interaction with my subconscious, while in hypnosis. My partner helped me find the programs my sub-conscious was running which kept me depressed. The sub-conscious always has a positive reason, often to protect us, for setting such behaviours up. But they're not always appropriate. Thankfully, we can consciously choose more helpful ways. Hypnotherapy gave me that choice. It allowed me to unhook those programs. These things are not logical, they're emotional and unique to every individual. It's not possible for me to tell anyone else what the cause of his or her depression, anxiety or any other problem might be. But each person's sub-conscious *always* knows. The gateway to freedom is right there, inside.

After the 'unhooking' work, while still in hypnosis, my partner asked me if there was anything else that needed attention. I was silent for a long time, because I was surprised by what popped straight into my head, and, given our relationship, I really wasn't sure what his reaction might be. Eventually, I asked, "What about love?" And my partner, who fortunately for me leaves his ego well out of the therapy, replied, "Well, Jan, you can give yourself all the love that you need."

Simple. We've all heard the idea that we need to love ourselves. But deep down do we know what that means? Do we give ourselves permission? Suddenly I had permission. My sub-conscious was working on it now.

I knew something had shifted, but it was a few days later that the lid came off. I felt like a leaden lid had been lifted from my heart. I felt like I was emitting a geyser of joy, from deep within me. From *inside* me. I was as high as a kite. This joy was emanating from a place so deep within me, it was *beyond* the body, it was from inner-space. It *had* to be from my soul.

In the space of a few weeks, I moved from rational-science-atheist to spiritual seeker. There is no doubt in my mind any longer that we are more than merely biology. We just need to get out of our own way, to allow ourselves to experience the joyous truth of that.

Every individual is free to find and embody that joy in their own way.

For me, it came as a profound realisation – no, a deep knowing and a felt experience – that I am connected to an infinite source of love that is everywhere, in everything. Indeed, it IS everything.

For me, joy and love are the same. I've been studying the language of that love, and how to bring more of it into my life experience, ever since. I know I'll never stop.

The path of love is the path of freedom. The rewards are amazing.

Happy Insights

Happy with the Universe

If you can develop an "attitude of gratitude" – being thankful for all that you have, rather than bemoaning what you lack – it will take you a long way down the road towards being happy every day.

I keep a "gratitude journal" where I write down a list of things I feel grateful for in that moment. They can be extraordinary things and very ordinary things. It's the first thing I do each morning, mug of tea in hand. It feels good to start the day that way. It doesn't feel like a chore, I look forward to it. I treat myself to a really pretty notebook to do it in, and it brings me a lot of pleasure.

Learning to be happy with uncertainty and change is very important in these times, when everything is changing so fast. Instead of bemoaning what life hands you, do your best to see everything as an opportunity, or at least as a welcome challenge. Eventually, we can learn to welcome even sad events and difficult circumstances for their ability to help us learn and grow.

It's helpful if we feel connected to others. Find ways to get involved in community, either locally with neighbours, by volunteering for a cause you feel passionate about or through common interest groups. It's amazing how that can increase your feeling that the world is a friendly place, rather than a frightening one.

Having a belief in a higher purpose provides immense comfort and this need not be through any particular religion. A new spirituality based on getting in touch with your own inner wisdom is growing and there is a wealth of information online, and in the Mind, Body, Spirit section of bookshops, to get you started.

I hope these pages will inspire you to seek a happy relationship with Life itself. I have learned to see my life as a beautiful gift which I cherish every day. I'm sure that you can do the same.

I see you, you shining light, and you are beautiful.

Shine on!

Tips for Loving Life

Well, I'm *certainly* no guru, but I'm on my way along a road where the sun is shinier every day (whatever the weather). I am now supremely happy with the universe and I'd like to share what I can of that with you.

There's no quick fix here, but every effort you make to put yourself on this path will bring you rewards you never could have imagined.

No 1: Acceptance

"Grant me the serenity to accept the things I cannot change, courage to change the things I can, and wisdom to know the difference"

Learning to discern the difference between the things we can change and the things we cannot is crucial to becoming happy with the universe. If we stop trying to do the impossible we are much more likely to be able to live a happy life.

Things you can change include your own moods, your own decisions, your own actions and the way you interact with other people. Things you cannot change are the moods of others, their decisions, their actions, the way they interact with people and pretty much everything else in the outside world.

That's not to say you're without influence; for example, you can reason with a loved one, you can request that they alter their behaviour. But you cannot actually cause that change to happen. Only they can make the change. And your success at influencing will be very dependent on how you go about it!

As for all the terrible things that go on in the world: you can't change them. You can change your actions, which undoubtedly makes a difference. You can drive more considerately. That's one more considerate driver on the road. You can shop more ethically. That's one less person funding unfair trading or pollution. You can donate. You can volunteer. You can write letters. You can demonstrate. You can have a quiet word with a work colleague or your boss. You can change what *you* do, but you cannot change anyone else's actions - they have the responsibility for that.

You cannot change the past. You can't go back to last week, last year, or to when you were a child, and do different then. You can only change how you feel about the past now. You can change your thoughts about it.

So: once you work out where that line is, accept all the things that happen over which you have no control. What is the point of getting upset or angry over those things? Accept them. If you're moved to action, change your behaviour in the ways that you can. But don't rail about things you cannot. That's like trying to push a mountain.

I like to refer to annoying people or circumstances as "environmental variables". It's like something in the landscape of your life that is there for you to negotiate, like a river you have to cross or a hill to climb. It would certainly be pointless to get upset about a river or a hill. They're just there. Stay cool, stay chilled, just find your way across or over. Or it's like the weather. Living in a temperate climate like England, I could be very miserable indeed if I let the weather bother me. We're as likely to get up to another cloudy day as a sunny one. Annoying people or circumstances are like clouds. Don't let them spoil your day. Be courteous yourself, maintain your equilibrium, hang on to your happy mood. Let them 'blow over'.

No 2: work on yourself

Are you serious about getting happy? Without getting all heavy about it, commit to doing whatever it takes to finding out how to become a happy person. As long as you're not hurting others, making yourself happy will benefit everyone.

For me, being happy with the universe hinges on being able, viscerally - in every part of my being - to understand this: my experience of Life - happy or unhappy, good or bad - comes not from what 'happens to me', but from my reactions to what happens.

This is good news, because - at least until we learn about who we really are and the universal laws governing Life - we often have no control over what happens to us, but we can learn to have control over our thoughts about events, and our reactions to them.

So, as Michael Bernard Beckwith says, "The Answer is You".

Read books, listen to audios, attend courses, search online, follow the tips in the other sections and keep learning until you get The Big Aha Moment over this one, because it is crucial.

If you're still saying, "I'll be happy when …" or "If only ….., then I could be happy…" you're not getting it. You're still expecting the solutions to come from outside of you.

Keep reading, keep trying. Even if it takes years, once you get it, you will be grateful for the time and effort you put in. The moment you understand this fully, your life will change forever. Like chains falling away. Like the cage door swinging open. Freedom beckons.

No 3: work on yourself … more!

Never stop learning. When you first begin, it seems difficult. After a while, it's like waking up from a trance, or from being half asleep. It's like getting up into the mountains where the air is clear and refreshing and the views are fantastic. Those who stay down in the valley have no idea of the beauty and majesty they are missing. Everyone can have this. They just have to get up and set out on the journey.

Hours of passive TV watching or reading sensationalist press dull the mind; it's what they're designed to do. You'll be amazed how excited you become about a new source of knowledge once you start feeding your mind good, nutritious information instead of the numbing 'fast food' churned out by conventional media.

Continued learning and expansion of your understanding about Life is what makes this journey so exciting and fulfilling.

There's no excuse for boredom. If you get bored, it's simply that you're not using your amazing power of imagination to create possibilities for yourself. Without exception your imagination is your greatest gift. Don't waste it. Michael Bernard Beckwith says that boredom is blocked creativity. So get unblocked and explore your magnificent Self.

No 4: connect with Life

Find your way to connect with the Energy that pulses through all Life. Call it the Divine, the Evolutionary Impulse, the Flow of Intention, the Universe, All That Is, Spirit, Source, the Force. Call it, if you wish to, God. Call it whatever you feel comfortable with, but think of it this way: it is in and through everything and everyone. It is energy. It is light. It is love.

We all are made of the same stuff. The Life that pulses in you, pulses in me too, and in everything in and on Earth, and in everything in this Galaxy and all others. Quantum physics is showing us what ancient wisdom has always taught: we are all connected at a very fundamental level. There is great joy in this connection.

So find your way to connect with this infinite source of joy and love, and you will understand that there is no need to look outside of your Self for happiness. It flows from within you, outward. From your personal joy generator.

For many people meditation is their way of connecting, for others it is being quiet in nature. Some may use yoga or other physical disciplines. For some it will be singing in a choir. Being creative, painting or sculpting or making music, is another route. If it fills you with joy, do more of it! Read about others' experiences. Don't limit yourself to one way, try a few until you find the combination to suit you.

If you are a convinced atheist you may find this step difficult to accept. That's OK. Do the things anyway. Meditation, for example, has scientifically documented physical, mental and emotional benefits. As does walking in nature! Just allow yourself to enjoy something where your mind is set free for a while.

No 5: connect with people

Do you think most people are selfish and rotten? Do you think people are scary? Or do you think people are fundamentally kind? If you have a negative view of humanity generally, I humbly suggest that you're hanging out with unhelpful types. You're in control of who you spend your time with. Don't blame anyone else, just take your precious time and spend it with people who help your spirits to lift.

Change your focus, start looking for the good in people. Good people to be with will then begin to show up for you.

Make the effort to smile at strangers, have a kind word with neighbours, get involved in community activities, join a choir, whatever takes your fancy. Get in touch with your Transition movement. Get out of your box and mix with people.

Find others who are searching for happiness too, others who are trying to learn a new way of being, and support each other in the process.

Connecting with people and having fun or solving problems together, or creating something together, is immensely satisfying and uplifting. And it cheers up your perspective on Life, the Universe and Everything, no end!

No 6: change your focus

Stop feeding your mind with negativity. TV news and the conventional press foster fear and dismay. Stop watching, stop reading. My life didn't fall over when I decided to do without them, four years ago. I haven't missed the TV at all, I'm too excited by all the other great things I can do with my time.

I keep myself informed through online news sources that I trust, and it is by no means all doom and gloom out there! Look for the positive things that are happening in the world, and you will surprise yourself at how much there is to celebrate. But don't expect conventional media to report it. Their function is not to cheer you up, their function is to feed you the corporations' propaganda and control you through fear, confusion and anxiety.

Cut down or cut out watching violent movies and reading novels about death and destruction. We know these things go on, but we don't have to indoctrinate ourselves with the horror of it. Find positive stories to lift you instead.

You're as much in control of what goes into your mind as what goes into your stomach. Learn to choose the good stuff. Happiness in, happiness out.

What you focus on is what shows up for you. Focus on negativity and the world will certainly hand you plenty that's bad. Focus on whatever you can find to cheer you, in any situation, and Life will begin sending you more and more of that.

No 7: gratitude

Always look for and celebrate what you can be grateful for. If you're in a bad situation, I'm sorry, I'm sending you all my love and my wishes that you can safely get out of it soon. But, hard though it might seem, do this anyway. Find something, anything, that you can feel grateful for, and keep your focus there. Practice gratitude. You will find yourself becoming happier, even though your circumstances haven't yet changed. Keep doing it.

A gratitude journal is one way to focus your attention on the positive things in life. Another way is to decide that whenever someone asks you how you are, you're going to tell them about something you're delighted with or thankful for, rather than your woes.

First you change your attitude, then, gradually, your circumstances will change. You will find the strength, out of your new perspective, to change your circumstances yourself.

Many blessings. I wish you the profound peace and deep joy of connecting with the Life Energy that animates all. I wish you great happiness for your time in this beautiful Universe.

What are the benefits that loving my life will bring me?

What values will loving my life satisfy?

My Cosmic Intentions

I am at peace with the universe.

I am loving Life.

I am enjoying the time that I am given.

Happy Ways Forward

A Word About Time

"There just isn't enough time"

"I don't have enough time"

"I wish I had more time"

Do you catch yourself saying this? Few of us are entirely free from those nagging phrases. I lived under their terrible pressure for years. I always had the haunting feeling, whatever I was doing, that maybe one of the other things on my 'to do' list was more urgent. I felt like time was chasing me, or I was chasing time. Or both, in ever decreasing circles.

Here's a lovely thought I had recently.

'What if ... we're *really* here to *savour* time?'

What if our purpose is to revel in this sensory experience, including our sense of time, to feed that information, that loving, grateful enjoyment of being here, back into the timeless, into the eternal, into the One?

As eternal beings of light and love, it's kind of funny (isn't it?) that we spend so very much of our gift of life running around feeling that we haven't enough time. Time, with sensory awareness, *IS* the gift!

How ludicrous that we should twist things around and get stressed by this exquisite gift. How typical. How human. Or is it? Perhaps it's more appropriate to say, how 'western'.

And if you don't believe you're eternal? If you think you get just this one chance and that's it? Even more crazy to go through this life in a frenzy.

Sensory awareness, our physical, breathing bodies, our relationships, our relatedness ... and our cognitive ability to ponder and celebrate these things ... these are the gifts of life, all meaningless without the sense of a linear progression, without time. Growing up and growing old. Sharing experiences.

I think the invitation here is for us to stop clamouring to the Cosmos that this beautiful gift of time is not enough - like a spoilt child with a glut of gifts at Christmas, hooked on opening presents and cataloging possessions but unable to enjoy any of them - and take responsibility for the time we have been given. To learn to work with and enjoy the subjectivity and elasticity of time. Learn to be effective with it, if we wish to be effective in life. Stop complaining that we don't have enough. We have a lifetime of it! It's up to us not to squander it. And it's perfectly within our power to research and then learn the ways that we can make our time more fulfilling.

Learn to love time. Love it, be filled with gratitude for it, savour it.

Time is *delicious*.

I wish you many joyous moments, where you have blissfully lost all track of time, because you are so immersed in doing what you love.

Snapshot: From Pushing to Pulling

I have a vision now of where I want to head. I have a map for, roughly, how to get there. And I have some guidelines for how I want to travel.

These are all based on my personal preferences. "Who better," declaims Abraham (through Esther Hicks), "than you, to get to decide your own preferences?" Who better, indeed? "... don't you realise, this is the evolution of all that we are?"

I feel that my goals, my plans, my direction and my way of getting there all now align with who I really am, with my soul's desires, and with my values. I'm no longer in conflict about my life path.

This means that instead of pushing or dragging myself to do things, I am pulled, drawn, inspired to get up and get on with the stuff of my day. I wish this for everyone. It is within everyone's grasp. Imagine a world like that! Imagine a world like that, and we will *make* it like that.

And that is the subject of my next little book: *Break Through the Clouds – your handy little guide to getting your life on track.*

Happy Adventuring!

More Happy Ways Forward

About Jan

I'm delighted to describe myself these days as a Life Enthusiast. I 'do' other stuff: I coach, I write, I photograph, I play in Photoshop, I paint, I design graphics, I build websites and teach others how to, I study, I'm training to be a hypnotherapist, I play my Irish bouzouki, I go for walks ... well, that gives you a picture, but does what I *do* define me? No, what defines me, as far as I'm concerned, is that I'm happy pretty much whatever I'm doing.

This book reflects my personal exploration of what happiness is and how to access it. My website features books, programs and products I've benefited from or that I'm drawn to right now. I've also provided a list of my favourite books in Further Reading, next.

My qualifications? I was deeply unhappy myself for a long time. Not any more! Step by step, I've moved myself from that sad state to feeling happy most of every day. I bounce back quickly from set-backs. I've let go of regrets about the past. I'm optimistic about the future. I'm feeling more and more fulfilled.

What I'm saying is, I know it's possible to shift into happiness as a way of being, rather than some distant goal, because I've done it. And I don't believe there's anything particularly special or unusual about me. Joy is something everyone can have, there is an infinite supply.

In fact, the more joy we feel, the more joy we spread! How great is that?

So here I'm sharing what I've learned personally, an introduction to what a host of experts in all areas of self-development and personal transformation can help you with as well.

I'm not suggesting that you need to take any of the ideas in this book 'as read', as Truth, as the best or the only way to get from where you are now to where you want to be. I am simply inviting you to try out as many of the ideas described here as catch your imagination.

If you find yourself feeling excited by the possibilities, you are on the right track! Excitement is our soul's navigation system. Follow your excitement, and you won't go far wrong.

Thank you for reading Break Through to Happiness. I hope you have enjoyed it, that you'll take a look at my website and that you find useful information every time you visit.

breakthroughtohappiness.co.uk

I wish you great joy in the next steps of your adventure.

Further Reading

Inspirational Books

Happy for No Reason by Marci Shimoff
Love for No Reason by Marci Shimoff
You'll See it When You Believe it by Dr Wayne W Dyer
The Power of Intention by Dr Wayne W Dyer
Excuses Begone by Dr Wayne W Dyer
The Seat of the Soul by Gary Zukav
Reinventing the Body, Resurrecting the Soul by Deepak Chopra
Dying to Be Me by Anita Moorjani
The Biology of Belief by Bruce Lipton
The Four Agreements by Don Miguel Ruiz
The Power of Now by Eckhart Tolle
A New Earth by Eckhart Tolle
The Answer is You by Michael Bernard Beckwith
The Field by Lynne McTaggart
The Bond by Lynne McTaggart
The Soul of Money by Lynne Twist
The Magician's Way by William Whitecloud
Transforming Stress by Doc Childre & Deborah Rozman
I am a Woman Finding my Voice by Janet F Quinn
The Impossible Just Takes a Little Longer by Art Berg
Leveraging the Universe & Engaging the Magic by Mike Dooley
Living with Joy by Sanaya Roman
Creating Money by Sanaya Roman & Duane Packer

More information, plus links through to useful websites, can be found on the Resources page of my website: **breakthroughtohappiness.co.uk**

Thank you so much for reading!

Keep smiling.

More Happy Insights

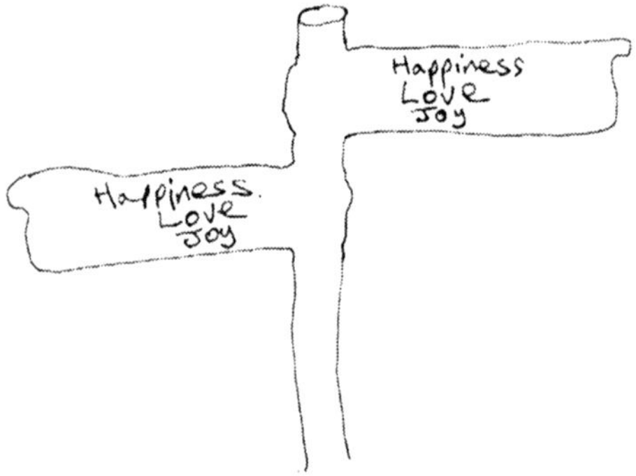

Lightning Source UK Ltd.
Milton Keynes UK
UKOW050814110713

213565UK00001B/17/P

9 781782 996729